from Sand Creek

from Sand Creek

**rising in this heart
which is our America**

by Simon J. Ortiz

Thunder's Mouth Press • Oak Park • New York

Published by Thunder's Mouth Press
242 W. 104th St. 5RW; New York, NY;
1152 S. East; Oak Park, IL.

Cover Painting by Robin Payne
Book & Cover design by Mary Beth Bostrom-Cybul

Grateful acknowledgement is made to *River Styx* and *Footprint Magazine* for poems previously published.

Funded in part by grants from the Illinois Arts Council and the Coordinating Council of Literary Magazines.

Library of Congress Cataloging in Publication Data

Ortiz, Simon J., 1941-
    From Sand Creek.

    I. Title.
PS3565.R77F7   811'.54   81-8795

ISBN 0-938410-03-2   AACR2
ISBN 0-938410-00-8 (pbk)

"Undying love," Danny said. Laughing, you have to.

For Danny, Billy, Nez, Larry, the Oklahoma Boy, Bingo, Ed, Apache, W., Ruidoso, Dusty, all those warriors

Other Books by Simon J. Ortiz:

Going For The Rain, poetry
A Good Journey, poetry
Howbah Indians, short stories
The People Shall Continue, poetry
Song, Poetry, and Language, essay bulletin
Fight Back: For The Sake of The People, For The Sake of The Land, poetry

Preface

A poet never knows how successful he is sharing his words — or how unsuccessful.

From Sand Creek is an analysis of myself as an American, which is hemispheric, a U.S. citizen, which is national, and as an Indian, which is spiritual and human. But in fact, it is all of these because the boundaries are not strictly defined and are not at all limiting. For one thing, I don't want them to be.

It is painful and frightening, as it should be, because I, as a poet, American and Indian, want my passionate love to be shared. I hope it is. The words from Sand Creek, from the land and people and some undefinable source in all of us, have been in their "creation" a music and prayer and discovery for me.

For Indian people, I would like *From Sand Creek* to be a study of that process which they have experienced as victim, subject, and expendable resource. For people of European heritage, I want it to be a study, too, but one which looks at motive and mission and their own victimization. I hope, finally, we will all learn something from each other. We must. We are all with and within each other.

Simon J. Ortiz
March 23, 1981

November 29, 1864: On that cold dawn, about 600 Southern Cheyenne and Arapaho People, two-thirds of them women and children, were camped on a bend of Sand Creek in southeastern Colorado. The People were at peace. This was expressed two months before by Black Kettle, one of the principal elders of the Cheyennes, in Denver to Governor John Evans and Colonel John W. Chivington, head of the Colorado Volunteers. "I want you to give all these chiefs of the soldiers here to understand that we are for peace, and that we have made peace, that we may not be mistaken for enemies." The reverend Colonel Chivington and his Volunteers and Fort Lyon troops, numbering more than 700 heavily armed men, slaughtered 105 women and children and 28 men.

A U.S. flag presented by President Lincoln in 1863 to Black Kettle in Washington, D.C. flew from a pole above the elder's lodge on that gray dawn. The People had been assured they would be protected by the flag. By mid-1865, the Cheyenne and Arapaho People had been driven out of Colorado Territory.

This America
has been a burden
of steel and mad
death,
but, look now,
there are flowers
and new grass
and a spring wind
rising
from Sand Creek.

Passing through, one gets caught into things; this time it was the Veterans Administration Hospital, Ft. Lyons, Colorado, 1974-75.

Grief
memorizes this grass.
Raw
courage,
         believe it,
red-eyed and urgent,
stalking Denver.
Like stone,
like steel,
the hone and sheer gone,
just the brute
and perceptive angle left.

Like courage,
         believe it,

left still;
the words from then
talk like that.

Believe it.

There was a trip we took once, and we all hid from the street's eyes and townspeople; you wouldn't believe we were this nation's children.

Toby is sick.
          Closely,
he looks after his shadow.

          Yes,
he is Indian.
He hides and tends
the shape of his face.
In the mirror
of Red & Bill's Cafe.
In La Junta.

He is impossible
to talk with then.
His frozen tongue
is frantic
          with prayer;
he wants to trust.

VA doctors tell him
not to worry.
That's his problem.

          His cough
is not the final blow,
but the glass wall
stares so closely.
Makes him afraid.

          Closely,
Toby tends his shadow.

Repression works like shadow, clouding memory and sometimes even to blind, and when it is on a national scale, it is just not good.

In 1969
XXXX Coloradoans
were killed in Vietnam.

In 1978
XXXX Coloradoans
were killed on the highways.

In 1864,
there were no Indians killed.

Remember My Lai.

In fifty years,
nobody knew
what happened.

It wasn't only the Senators.

Remember Sand Creek.

It was a national quest, dictated by economic motives. Europe was hungry for raw material, and America was abundant forest, rivers, land.

Many of them
built their sod houses
without windows.
Without madness.

But fierce, o
with a just determination.

Consulting axioms
and the dream called America.

Cotton Mather was no fool.

A few remembered
Andrew Jackson,
knew who he was,
ruminating, savoring
fresh Indian blood.

Style is a matter
of perference,
performance,
judgement yearning
to be settled quickly.

The axiom
would be the glory of America
at last,
            no wastelands,
no forgiveness.

The child would be sublime.

Autumn is beautiful in Colorado, like a golden dusk, rich with smell, the earth settling into a harvest, and one could feel like a deep story.

Words stumble
on October stories,
the abrupt wind
throttled
              on fences
barn slats
              spikes
thudding
bad cast iron.

A last magpie
nods
an ancient
bitter nod.

Strangers,
they accept us
afterall
as afternoon travellers
our mission
unknown to them.

The magpie is determined
to freeze.

Buffalo were dark rich clouds moving upon the rolling hills and plains of America. And then the flashing steel came upon bone and flesh.

Acres
across which to run.

Who forsook
these ones?

A cow stolen
from her memory,
the wild breed
            of Europe
            of Africa
            of Asia,
does not agitate
the weak fence.

Buffalo ghosts
hurdle away.

           No gentle sigh
to cling to.

They rode like steel,
blades flashing.

Sighs sighs weave grass.

Who watches now?

There was a recurrent dream for a while of driving east, passing near Sand Creek; tension was a tight string straight as the Kansas border.

Sky is panned
concave,
the eyeballs
                blanch.

Memory
is shriven
clean
as Kansas stateline.
We approached
                winter.

Memory
is stone, very quiet,
like this,
a moment clenched tightly
as knuckles
around gunstock
around steering wheel.

By the year 1901, only a few Utes were left in Colorado. Early as November,
clouds can't do anything but put their backs to the wind, follow
the highway east and then south.

Summer cheats
leaves —
you think like that
unwelcomed
inappropriate — season
feels like
it's up for grabs.
Discontinuance.
     Winter sun
abrupts,
though on course,
clouds broken
like bad asphalt,
clumsy curbs.
     Cold,
it is,
the wind lurches
blunt and sad.
Below freezing in Colorado.

Ghosts Indian-like
still driven
towards Oklahoma.

W. and Nez sat upon the dike ridge, singing; east and south lay endless plains and low hills, and to the west of them rose the Rockies. Land and sky; flowers and generations.

You

ought to have
heard them cry

         singing
summoning eternity,
the fools.

Singing,
longing,
reluctance.

Flowers are delicate,
they are,

       these generations
still sing forth,
crying.

     Aaiiieee.

Stuck them on their caps
and called.

Did not know how
they were patriots.

Conquest reached Nevada: a warrior chief was assassinated by the cavalry,
cut into stewing pieces, fed to other chiefs, and a Treaty was signed.
That'll show 'em. Ask the Paiutes.

Violence is even
beautiful.

        Mastery
of pain
is crucial
to this work.

A senator
did not need to hawk
Biblical phrases.

           It was
all ordained and certain.

They clamored for salvation,
those stalwart victims
sent
as messengers,
already avengers
fore-running justice,

to Colorado.

Even the farmer has become a loser; in small Kansas, Iowa, Nebraska towns, there are more bars than churches or food stores.

Dreams
thinned
and split
can only produce
these bones.

            The last outpost
known,
the rusted plowshare.

Talked to a farmer
about Arapaho schemes.
They knew things
were too good to last,
said he.

      In Denver,
I could drink them under
the table anytime.

All they remembered
was open plain and mountains.
They wouldn't even/couldn't even
consider Denver anyway.

Me,
I think as far as California,
I do.

In this hemisphere, corn is ancient and young; it is the seed, food, and symbol of a constantly developing and revolutionary people.

Don't fret now.

Songs are useless
to exculpate sorrow.
That's not their intent anyway.

Strive
for significance.
Cull seeds from grass.
Develop another strain of corn.

Whisper for rain.

Don't fret.
Warriors will keep alive in the blood.

Pain and death did not have to be propagated as darkness and wrong and coldness; they could have listened and listened and learned to sing in Arapaho.

Somehow
it was impossible
for them
to understand true safety.

Knowledge for them
was impossible
to understand as pain.
That was untrustworthy,
lost to memory.

Death was sin.

Their children
hunkered down, frightened
into quilts, listening
to wind
speaking Arapaho words
for pain and beauty and generations.

But they refused to understand.
Instead, they protested
the northwind,
kept adding rooms.
Built fences.
Their children learned to plan.
Their parents required submission.

Warriors could have passed
into their young blood.

La Junta: in this town, we are not dangerous anymore, and the townspeople know it; they volunteer nothing, no compassion, no love.

Violence
upon these,

                    especially the white
                    ones, ordinary men,
is vivid.

They just don't know anymore.
That's all.
They are soothed by it.
Their only comfort and safety.

We left
this morning.
They know us.
                    They knew
we would be mad,
and so they gave us plenty.
Little paper cups
so full of knowledge.

And now,

            we're free
                to wander, lost.
To seek for safe shadows
that will remind us
of what we knew before.
But we will not yearn.
So full of knowledge.

                    Even
the town's young toughs
do not mess with us.

                    We are glazed
with war.
They can smell the sour
and the glisten
                of our sweat.

Violence is easy and good.

Free and hollow, a cold glistening.

You can't help but be American, not a citizen or a shadow but a patriot and warrior for land and people even when insignificant and lost.

La Junta:
        they let us
        be mad
in their town.

My partners, hollows
        and pockets,
are shadows
        of souls.
But souls nevertheless.

We park on a side street,
do not draw attention,
and wander away,
        shuffling.

I drift
    away
as shadow,

anonymous, not willing
to be mad.

        Nonetheless,
        nonetheless,
I am their partner. Them.

It's almost inexplicable that Black Elk would say the dream ended; we know why now, and we know it did not and will not end.

Bones
are no longer
stark reference.

We don't study horizons
as necessity
anymore.

Last signs.

One, or two, several soldiers
swiftly
expertly
at her
        self her generations

uuh aaieee
            uh

'oh susianna don't
you cry for me'

Stuck them
on their hats to dry.

Their fingers greasy
and slick.

There are ghost towns all over the West; some are profitable tourist attractions of the "frontier," others are merely sad and unknown.

What should have been
important and fruitful
became bitter.
       Wasted.
       Spots appeared on their lungs.
       Marrow dried
           in their bones.
       They ranted.
Pointless utterances.
Truth did not speak for them.

It is a wonder
they even made it to California.

But, of course,
they did,
and they named it success.
Conquest.
Destiny.

Frontiers ended for them
and a dread settled upon them
and became remorseless
           nameless
           namelessness.

In the VAH, you can't be anything but alien to the combat soldiers if you don't know the glaze and sour sweat; all Billy would talk about was going to Kansas City and freedom.

Arkansas River is turgid
and sorrowful blood.

I point that out to Maguire.

But he doesn't listen.
His nights are bad dreams.
Not always, but lately.

The VA psychologist
tells him to tell them.

They try to frighten us
with their madness
but we know better.
Billy wasn't always alien.

Finally, he listens.

Look Billy, stories
are reliable as those river stones.

They were fierce, Billy,
atrocious, shiny blades glistening
in the cold sun,
you could smell their sour sweat.

As we walk back,
he tells me his secret plan:
head east for Kansas, make arrows.
Send word to the IRA.

Indian astronomers studied the stars and set them in their memory so their people would not ever forget their place in all creation. What did Copernicus think?

They crossed country
that would lay
beyond memory.

Their cells
would no longer bother
to remember.
                    Memory
was not to be trusted.

They had plans.
Fortuitous for those
who had designs.

They had plans
but they could have
matched the land
                    like those
who had searched
the plains and tied themselves
to stars,
      insects,
      generations and generations,
instinct
for millenia.

When they didn't,
star light fractured,
became unpredictable.

Aimlessly,
they crossed memory.

Whiskey was only one way and guns another; it was a scheme that did it: scare them, make them dependent and hopeless, sell them anything, tell them it's for their own good.

The traders who dealt
in whiskey
came

       imploring
a false trust
so thorough

and sincere
even Black Kettle
did not turn away;

he withered

like a dying root.

          Even winter
knows no such sorrow.

Whiskey end.
Poisoned.

Who stole the hearts and minds of the humble hard-working folk until they too became moralistic and self-righteous: senators, bishops, presidents, missionaries, corporation presidents?

They were simple enough.
Swedes, Germans,
Mennonites, Dutch,
Irish, escaping
Europe.
          Running.

They shouldn't have stopped
and listened to Puritans.
And learned
that mountains were chains
to be crossed like breaking
something.

They should have eaten
whole buffalo.
They should have,
like the People wanted for them.

They shouldn't have listened
to those strange preachers.
The Congress. Cotton Mather.
On their way west.

They shouldn't have understood
those Biblical words that way
and become simple as death.
And, finally, complex liars.
          And thieves.

Colonel Chivington was a moral man, believed he was made in the image of God, and he carried out the orders of his nation's law; Kit Carson didn't mind stealing and killing either.

At the Salvation Army
a clerk
caught me
wandering
among old spoons
 and knives,
  sweaters and shoes.

I couldn't have stolen anything;
my life was stolen already.

In protest though,
I should have stolen.
My life. My life.

She caught me;
Carson caught Indians,
secured them with his lies.
Bound them with his belief.

After winter,
our own lives fled.

I reassured her
what she believed.
Bought a sweater.

And fled.

I should have stolen.
My life. My life.

There is a revolution going on; it is very spiritual and its manifestation is economic, political, and social. Look to the horizon and listen.

The mind is stunned stark.

At night,
Africa is the horizon.

The cots of the hospital
are not part of the dream.

Lie awake, afraid.
Thinned breath.

Was it a scream again.
                    Far
below, far below,
the basement speaks
for Africa, Saigon, Sand Creek.

Souls gather
around campfires.
Hills protect them.

Mercenaries gamble
for odds.
            They'll never know.
Indians stalk beyond the dike,
carefully measure the distance,
count their bullets.

Stark, I said,
stunned night in the VAH.

Women and men may be broken and scattered, but they remember and think about the reasons why. They answer their own questions and always the truth and love will make them decide.

Nez wanted to break in.
He had confessed,
I could have killed,
maybe I did.
W., the Sioux,
blunted his fingers
                    on the wall.
Kit Carson Chapel at Ft. Lyons.
You know, we stood shivering
to some kind of error
that afternoon.

We could have become
warriors again, rounded
up the maniacs, made them hush.

High up, the stained glass
blazed, fireless.

W. didn't know it
when he spoke soft fire,
But love, that's reasonable,
we're people, not like them.

Scholasticism and intellectualism have been barriers to emotion. No wonder there is such a fear of women, children, blood and anger: control them.

Anger meant nothing to them,
not even as intellectual exercise.
Their scholars set them
away from it
              and deemed
that they should be systematic.
Exclusive.

              And so deliberate
that their intellect
became foreign to them.

They were frightened by emotion.
The sheer joy of being men,
of being children,
was no longer theirs.
They feared women.

Their scholars deemed —
                       no,
ordained —
that they would be trivial
as their blood diminished.
But, yes,
they could have been important.

They should have seen
the thieves stealing
their most precious treasure:
their compassion, their anger.

This swirl of America has a special mystique that we have been sold,
but look north, west, south, east, all around; it is ours to know.

Looking for Billy,
I knew he wasn't anywhere
nearby.

      Like his words,
he could be anywhere.

He was gone,
      west,
south, east,
      anywhere.

He was the shadow.

Memory was his lost trail.

West, then south, then east,
a swirl of America
in his brain.

Looking for shadow,
he could be anywhere.

The veterans hospital, like other U.S. institutions, has the same hierarchy as the Church and State; it has no more authority than brute persuasion and force.

The Texan
who takes care of the coffee pot,
who is my vice-president,
is confused by why
I am so mad
with love for these derelicts
who come to us
asking for tobacco, coffee,
shaving cream, shoe laces.

He bludgeons me with his stare.

But I look into his exile eyes,
flaunt my authority,
which he understands,
and I give them what they beg
and apologize for.

        Coffee.
        Cigarettes.
        Shaving cream.
Shoe laces.

I am innocently American afterall,
generous, guileless,
            but
it is the aboriginal
and the savage that cringes
under his murderous eyes,
and I have to move away
from the invisible gesture
of his hand reaching for my throat.

The derelicts and I
trade poor comfort, receive,
shuffle, and dodge the exile.

The Polka Dot Kid said, "I was born dirt poor and religious in Raton, New Mexico and forty-two years later I found myself in a skidrow hotel in Amarillo; I thought I was in Denver."

Deranged,
they were frantic
enough.
            Never thought
that guilt was a partner.
Why?
            No reason to feel so.

They burned it
and their minds like rags.

Weather, they reasoned,
is to be shielded against.
Children were to be ordered.
Future meant effort, hoarding.

Denver was a camp
of tents in 1861.

The mirage would not fade.

Easily enough,
the wagons came on;

the horizon fell behind
without trace of memory.

Just like they came,
civilized, souless.

The blood poured unto the plains, steaming like breath on winter mornings; the breath rose into the clouds and became the rain and replenishment.

They were amazed
at so much blood.
                    Spurting,
                        sparkling,
splashing, bubbling, steady
hot arcing streams.
                    Red
and bright and vivid
unto the grassed plains.
                    Steaming.

So brightly and amazing.
They were awed.

It almost seemed magical
that they had so much blood.
It just kept pouring,
like rivers,
like endless floods from the sky,
thunder that had become liquid,
and the thunder surged forever
into their minds.

                    Indeed,
they must have felt
they should get on their knees
and drink the red rare blood,
drink to replenish
their own vivid loss.

Their helpless hands
were like sieves.

Like many other Americans, I love movies, and there were movies at the Veterans Hospital. Watching, men and boys throbbed and ached, passionately, hopelessly.

Dusty plays
the piano
before the movie begins.
His fingers blunt
themselves upon keys.
          Throbbing
bullets and aches.

He is mute otherwise.
Memory for him
rattles in dry cells.

Dusty, Dusty, play
for us
before the movie begins.

He plays and his tears
are no music.
          Throbbing aches
and bullets.

If patriotism made any sense, because it was necessary, you would think they wouldn't throw anybody away. There was this Colonel.

Even this one,
this Colonel
as everyone calls him,
they reject.
He grew giddy with patriotism,
but in his own way
he is a brand of renegade
you can detect
in the shadow
                    of his face.

He wonders why, of course,
why they drove him here.
For him, a last resort,
a rejection unclear to him
who served them.

Millionaires
would reward him with solace,
one would think,
                    bedeck him
with medals and admiration.
But no,
they cast him, soulfirst,
here, a whirlpool
of exiles drowning him.

Men and war and fortune and destiny — the real winner and culprit is the imperial one; the agents and men are only agents and men.

Billy and Danny and Larry. And me.
We all thought we might be winners
at any moment.

                    We wandered
over to Casino Night in a building
which commanded by its appearance.
But it was nothing
if it wasn't an Army past and ghost.

Before and after,
there are Army
and appointed agents creeping
among us, guiding us
to destinies which are not ours.

Larry said Hello to an old man
from World War II and Ward D
who was numb with experience;
for him reality is now no more.

Larry guided him through the door
which was not a door for him
into Casino Night and Danny
held the door in its hinge.
Larry smiled Right On
and Billy, he smiled too.

The old man knew he would not win.
He was as fortunate as all of us.

Dreams are so important because they are lifelines and roadways, and nobody should ever self-righteously demean or misuse them.

If they could have
dreamed untroubled
and gentle dreams,
dreams would have been roads.
Instead, self-righteousness
became a necessary style
for breathing, and breathing
self-righteously they deemed
themselves blessed and pure
so that not even breath
became life —
                life strangled
                in their throats.

        Blood
gurgled and ran backwards
and swirled them into a whirl
of greed and callousness.
And this very dream crossed
rivers and burned forests
and scarred futures.
Hot steam poured
from red frantic mouths.

There is probably no way to verify if people become self-righteous and arrogant because they are dissatisfied or failures, but they certainly do.

They must have felt
no need to know anything
eternal.
       Anything
was true enough,
good enough for them.
Wild animals, wild rivers,
and wildness was not foreign
to them but they only heard
frantic warning whispers
of hungry starved European ghosts.
And they created new ghosts
as they needed them.

And onward,
          westward
they marched,
sweeping aside the potential
of dreams which could have been
generous and magnificent
and genius for them.

        It is
no wonder
they deny regret
for the slaughter
of their future.
Denying eternity, it is no wonder
they became so selflessly
righteous.

The land and Black Kettle took them in like lost children, and by 1876 land allotment and reservations and private property were established.

They must have known.

                     Surely,
they must have.
              Black Kettle
met them at the open door
of the plains.

             He swept his hand
all about them.
The vista of the mountains
was at his shoulder.
                 The rivers
run from the sky.
              Stone soothes
every ache.
           Dirt feeds us.
Spirit is nutrition.
           Like a soul, the land
was open to them, like a child's heart.
There was no paradise,
but it would have gently and willingly
and longingly given them food and air
and substance for every comfort.
If they had only acknowledged
even their smallest conceit.

When I was younger — and America was young too in the 19th century — Whitman was a poet I loved, and I grew older. And Whitman was dead.

O Whitman
spoke for them,
of course,
        but he died.
That shed their sorrow
and shame
and cultured their anxiety.
They spoke an eloquent arrogance
by which they thought
they would be freed.
In their theaters,
in their factories,
in their wars.
        They wasted
their sons and uncles
as they came westward,
sullenly insisting
that perhaps, O Whitman,
O Whitman, he was wrong
and had mis-read the goal
of mankind.
        And Whitman
who thought they were his own—
did he sorrow?
did he laugh?
Did he, did he?

Thunder rolling across the plains is a beautiful valorous noise,
but the train that became America roars and cries.

The sky is brilliant
and expansive like the universe
on the concave of my eye.
My mind is a cove
                    of light
shining upon a vista
of a grassed great plain.
I know
there is a world
peopled with love.
I know
there are people
                    who speak
not in undertones
but gallantly and joyously,
who are valorous
with simple courage.
But looking at the VA hospital
fortressed with dike walls
in defense against the rising
Arkansas River, I see
a train that carries dreams
and freedom away.

                    Thunder rises
in me and its waves empty me.
                    O
train and people and plains,
look at me and the hospital
where stricken men and broken boys
are mortared and sealed
into its defensive walls. O look,
now.

There is an honest and healthy anger which will raze these walls, and it is the rising of our blood and breath which will free our muscles, minds, spirits.

There was a man
who cried
            for his mother.
His anger
was so ferocious it rang
and cracked
through the hospital
walls.
            My own
throat constricted.
            And my
shoulders hunched
            in secret.
I could have flown
through the wall
his anger had opened.
And strangled him
to soothed finality.
But my own dread,
his own mother,
my own muscles refused
the wings needed.
I could only cry,
                  mangled
like his anger,
amazed
and dismayed.

The future will not be mad with loss and waste though the memory will be there; eyes will become kind and deep, and the bones of this nation will mend after the revolution.

Probably,
they didn't know
that walls
would be constructed,
that wars were to make
these men possible.
That there
would be a time
when eyes would grow shallow,
when bones were to be broken,
when eardrums would be shattered,
and the final atomic waste swept
into piles and used
to estimate futures.
But then, they did not think,
they would have survived
if they did not know arrogance
and would have to share reports
of history which now rise
before us as mutant generations.

We all called him Apache. They said all he did was carry out orders in Korea. The only thing he ever talked about was dawn at Dulce and freedom, just like Billy.

There should be
moments of true terror
that would make men think
and that would cause women
to grab hold of children,
loving them, and saving them
for the generations
who would enjoy the rain.
        Who are
these farmers,
who are these welders,
who are these scientists,
who are those soldiers
with cold flashing brilliance
and knives.
            Who struck aside
the sacred dawn
and was not ashamed
before the natural sun and dew?
Artistically,
they splattered blood
along their mad progress;
they claimed the earth
and stole hearts and tongues
from buffalo and men,
the skilled
butchers, aerospace engineers,
physicists they became.
The future should hold them
secret, hidden and profound.

It was they, ambitious and greedy, who made an angry god because they rejected and envied something they couldn't control; so they were the ones who lost Billy. They became shallow eyes too.

The excuse is easy:
my father did not know.

Love should be answerable for.
The responsibility of being enjoined.
But God did not possess these.
Instead, he lingered
like a fugitive who thundered
wrath and vengeance
at the edge of the crowds
burning women in Salem.

Andrew Jackson claimed Him.
He made his slave women bear
his children for profit.
And the fugitives crossed
land and rivers
and swept their trails clean
forever from their memory.

Their minds became technical
and able and foresighted,
looking towards Asia, Africa,
the Mideast, Brazil.

              Just yesterday,
they returned them
to their mothers,
but they were shallow eyes
called men.
        Billy?
        Billy?

I have always loved America; it is something precious in the memory in blood and cells which insists on story, poetry, song, life, life.

In the Dayroom,
the Oklahoma Boy sits
sunken into the arms
of a wooden and leather couch
that has become his body.
The structure of his life
and the swirl of his mind
have become lead.

There is beauty
in his American face,
but the dread implanted
by the explosive
in Asia denies it.
The life he now matters by
is pushed away without pity
by the janitors broom
which strikes his shoe.
Only the corners
of his eyes and the edge
of his shoe know the quality
of the couch he has become.

It is the life he has submerged
into, a dream needing a name.
He has become the American,
vengeful and a wasteland
of fortunes, for now.

That dream
shall have a name
after all,
and it will not be vengeful
but wealthy with love
and compassion
and knowledge.
And it will rise
in this heart
which is our America.

About the Author

Simon J. Ortiz was born in Albuquerque, New Mexico and raised in the Acoma Pueblo community. He was schooled formally within the Bureau of Indian Affairs, state, and Catholic education systems, but he insists that the experience of the Indian in America has been his real education. He was a student of several colleges including Ft. Lewis College, University of New Mexico, and the University of Iowa where he was a Fellow in the International Writing Program. He has taught Native American Literature and Creative Writing at San Diego State University, Navajo Community College, Marin College, Institute for the Arts of the American Indian, and the University of New Mexico. Author of *Going For The Rain; A Good Journey; Howbah Indians; The People Shall Continue; Song, Poetry, and Language,* he is currently working on a collection of short stories and a novel. Presently, he lives in Albuquerque; he has two children, Raho Nez and Rainy Dawn.